The Art of Teaching Online

The Art of Teaching Online

How to Start and How to Succeed as an Online Instructor

Larry Cooperman

ELSEVIER

CP
CHANDOS PUBLISHING
An imprint of Elsevier

Chandos Publishing is an imprint of Elsevier
50 Hampshire Street, 5th Floor, Cambridge, MA 02139, United States
The Boulevard, Langford Lane, Kidlington, OX5 1GB, United Kingdom

British Library Cataloguing-in-Publication Data
A catalogue record for this book is available from the British Library

Library of Congress Cataloging-in-Publication Data
A catalog record for this book is available from the Library of Congress

ISBN: 978-0-08-101013-6 (print)
ISBN: 978-0-08-101120-1 (online)

For information on all Chandos Publishing publications
visit our website at https://www.elsevier.com/books-and-journals

Publisher: Glyn Jones
Acquisition Editor: Glyn Jones
Editorial Project Manager: Jennifer Pierce
Production Project Manager: Debasish Ghosh
Cover Designer: MPS

Typeset by MPS Limited, Chennai, India

DEDICATION

Once more, to my wife Adrienne, with all my love.

CONTENTS

INTRODUCTION

The cost of a college education, over the last few decades, has outpaced the inflation rate several times over. Easily available student loans have left many students drowning in debt, many with academic degrees that cannot help them find employment. Higher education institutions have been saddled with numerous regulations that result in even higher tuition for students. Higher education is at a crossroads, especially in the United States and Western Europe, but developing countries, such as India and Brazil, require education systems that allow for large numbers of students to study successfully at a low cost. What is the solution here for higher education at the beginning of the 21st century?

There is not one answer, not one panacea, that can solve the issue of mass higher education at a reasonable cost, but in the last decade, online education has been touted by many people as one solution to the growing need of making education affordable to all at a decent cost. The rise of massive open online courses (MOOCs), fueled by advances in technology such as ubiquitous Internet access and online education software platforms such as Engage by companies such as Udacity and Coursera, have the potential to make the idea of education for all a reality. Despite objections by those in academia who believe online education is not as effective a platform as the traditional classroom lectures that have existed since the time of Plato, recent actions, such as the successful cohort completion of an online master's degree in computer science from the Georgia Institute of Technology, demonstrate that MOOCs and other forms of online education, such as webinars, are here to stay and will coexist with traditional education, or perhaps supplant traditional education models. Other types of online education, such as webinars for continuing education in numerous professional fields, have made learning much more convenient and accessible for millions of people.

The point again to make here is that online education, for all its advantages and disadvantages, is not going away from the education world, and that online education also contains many potential uses for all sorts of education delivery and learning around the world. Online education also allows for instructors who might not, in the past, have considered teaching or been able to teach students at the postsecondary level. Most teaching positions at this level of education usually required a PhD and a tenure track position at a traditional brick-and-mortar university. With the advent of online education, professionals who hold a master's degree and relevant work experience can now teach undergraduate students online; the advent of this trend allows those with the requisite academic background to also provide much-needed expertise from their occupations and professional experience. This is not to denigrate the traditional PhD professors who teach and teach their students effectively; what online education does is to allow those holders of an advanced degree (but not the most advanced degree) with crucial real-world skills to pass those skills on to their students. Professionals who may have wanted to teach in a postsecondary setting in the past can now do so, thanks to the growing presence of online education in the postsecondary education field.

I have taught online research and report writing courses for the past five years, and I discovered that I not only enjoyed teaching undergraduate students online, but I also learned organizational and writing skills that I did not possess before I began teaching. The college where I teach provided me with an excellent orientation to online teaching, but I thought, over the years that I have taught, that others new to online teaching, professionals with a master's or doctoral degree, could use a manual that will guide them to a successful career in online education. This book will serve as such a handbook for those who are new to the field and who wish to learn skills that will enable them to become successful online educators. There are many books available that provide an excellent pedagogical background for successful online instruction; this book will have more of a personal emphasis from my own experience as an online instructor, and will also focus on the importance of the art of mastering online education, and of maintaining the personal touch of an instructor in an online world. **Interviews with online instructors will also be a major feature of this handbook.** One major criticism of online education is its impersonal nature; with this book, I hope to provide the emphasis on enhancing the human element to make online education more personable to the online student. Online education may not entirely replace traditional education, but this book hopes to make online education a personable and successful endeavor to those who wish to teach students online.

CHAPTER 1

So You Want to Teach Online

The Art of Teaching Online. DOI: http://dx.doi.org/10.1016/B978-0-08-101013-6.00001-1

When I tell people that I teach online, I usually receive two general responses. The first is amazement and wonder—what's it like to teach online? How do the students learn? What technologies do you use? The other response is that online education is so impersonal; why would I want to teach students I couldn't see or talk with? I usually answer that online education (for the rest of this book, "online education" will deal with postsecondary education) may seem, at first glance, distant, formal, and impersonal, but this rapidly evolving form of education also allows for personal interaction and, as an online instructor for five years, I strive to provide as much personal interaction as I can, given the constraints of a computer. In fact, I am more comfortable teaching in front of a computer than in a lecture hall, having spent more than a half-decade teaching undergraduates online, as well as teaching librarians continuing education courses (most of which I have created). And technologies such as live classroom lecture platforms allow for a more personable online education experience. I am very fortunate to work for a school whose goal is to provide the most personable online education experience, and their embrace of technologies to accomplish this is very wise and helpful.

What are the benefits of an online education? Price is probably the major benefit—most schools (but not all of them, unfortunately) can lower their tuition if they can teach more students at a given time. This is the theory underlying the popularity of massive online open courses (MOOCs) at large universities; they can educate a large number of students for a lower price than a traditional college education, and can offer free or low-cost education to nonmatriculated students.

Another major benefit of an online education is its flexibility and portability—of course, the semester or quarter system of scheduling classes will not change, but the ability to study, to learn, to listen to live classroom lectures, and to take examinations anyplace, anywhere, and at any time is a great boon for those who work and attend classes. Online students are not tied to a lecture hall or a study hall; for them, anyplace with a Wi-Fi hotspot *is* their lecture hall and their study hall. And the availability of numerous online subject databases and e-books allow students unparalleled access to research resources from any location; students do not need to set foot on a college campus and still receive a quality education. Many of today's students work full time, have attended some college courses in the past, or need to return to school to earn a degree for their profession; these students do not need the traditional, ivy-covered campus amenities of a cafeteria, student union, and football games. This is not to say that the traditional college route is dying; what is occurring, courtesy of 21st century technology, is an alternative to a very expensive education over a four-year period, which may even be shortened due to shorter, accelerated classes that still provide a quality education. Many of today's students need a practical, relatively inexpensive education to fulfill their needs, and online education increasingly fits those needs efficiently and effectively.

The explosion of online education in the last few years has required schools to hire more instructors, primarily those holding a master's degree or higher. Many of these positions, granted, are adjunct positions and are not always full time positions, which is the desired goal for many educators, given that many educational institutions cannot afford to pay online instructors benefits for full time positions. Nevertheless, many professionals already do work full time, or have other work that provides additional income, so starting an adjunct faculty position in online education is not a monetary or work issue for most professionals.

Looking beyond the monetary aspect of online instructor positions, why should a professional become an online instructor (or faculty member, as these phrases can be loosely interchanged)? The desire to impart a professional's experience and expertise in a given field to students eager to learn new skills, the desire to learn new skills from teaching students, the ability to learn new technologies, mainly from learning management systems (LMSs) and electronic lecture software such as Adobe Connect or Cisco WebEx. Speaking for myself, I had wanted to teach online for a very long time (close to 10 years). I believed that my research and writing skills as a librarian would allow me to teach these skills to undergraduates in a postsecondary setting; many librarians teach students information literacy in college or teach their colleagues in a continuing education setting, whether live or online. I had taught in both of these areas, and originally rejected teaching online. But five years ago, I had another chance to do so, and immediately accepted the position—and I have not regretted it. I had skills that could be taught online to students who needed those critical thinking, research, and writing skills to succeed in their careers, and I had the background in teaching information literacy and library continuing education to allow me to succeed online.

This leads to a self-assessment: do you, a successful professional who wants to learn new skills and to work in a new environment, believe you can become a successful online instructor? Think about how much experience you have gained and developed in your professional field; there is no specific yardstick to how much experience you need to have accumulated in your field, of course, but if you believe you have skills and experience that you can impart and relate to students, then you will succeed as an online instructor. Remember that these skills and experience cover a wide array of professions; information technology and healthcare are very popular educational fields, but online educational institutions will always need mathematicians, English instructors, and other general education instructors in addition to specific business or healthcare instructors.

Once you have decided that you know you have enough professional experience to begin as an online instructor, think about if you can devote enough time to successfully teach an online course (or courses), given your work schedule and other commitments. I usually teach two or three courses each semester, some six weeks and some the entire 11 weeks of a semester, and I average about 20 hours per week teaching my online courses. This includes reading assignments, grading, and preparing and delivering weekly online lectures; with my courses, my students do not take quizzes or examinations (they have to submit final projects), but if your subject matter involves quizzes and examinations, as many do, you will need to factor additional teaching time into your schedule. Think about your organizational and time management skills as well; successful online instructors, based on their years of experience in their fields, are able to prioritize and balance several tasks or projects at one time. Your students could (and probably will) bombard you with email messages, instant messages, or texts for guidance on how to finish their homework, projects or reports; a successful online instructor needs to be able to have ample time to promptly respond to their students' questions, as well as to have as much of an online presence as possible. It is obvious that a successful online instructor needs to have a good deal of skills and experience to successfully teach online students; some not-so-obvious, but crucial, skills for a successful online instructor to have are empathy, understanding, and a human presence behind an electronic computer screen, an emotional intelligence and understanding to ensure that their students succeed.

Online education is not for everyone; it is not a panacea to solve the educational needs of students around the world. But online education, for the right students and the right instructors, can be an enriching and enlightening educational source, where they both learn skills and experience that can help them succeed in the world.

CHAPTER 2

Additional Self-Assessments and Getting Started With Online Instruction

The Art of Teaching Online. DOI: http://dx.doi.org/10.1016/B978-0-08-101013-6.00002-3

ADDITIONAL SELF-ASSESSMENTS

Now that you have made a start at a self-assessment on if you will become a successful online instructor, you need to make some additional self-assessments. If the first set of self-assessments dealt with your skills in your professional area, what other skills do you need to become a successful online instructor?

The next set of skills deal with instruction and teaching itself—this book is not meant to become a handbook of online teaching pedagogy, but there are several general aspects of instruction that will provide a good self-assessment for successful online instruction; these aspects will be discussed at more length later in this book.

What is the final remaining aspect of online instruction that needs a self-assessment? That is the proficiency of using various technological online instruction tools. The main technological tools online instructors use is the web-based teaching platform commonly called the learning management system (or LMS). Many common LMSs are Moodle-based or Blackboard-based; it usually is not a prerequisite to have experience using these systems before beginning instruction, but a professional can gain experience with them by using them if they do teach continuing education courses online, as I have done in the past (which accounts for my experience using Moodle-based platforms). However, these systems are very easy to use and to navigate, and require only patience and an open, curious mind to use them successfully.

Other technological tools include live lecture-based platforms, such as Adobe Connect or Cisco's WebEx, and tools to create and to embed videos in either PowerPoint presentations or in classroom lectures (such as EyeJot or Vimeo). Many professionals have used these tools in their work, so many should be familiar enough to use them in an educational setting. Whether or not a potential online instructor has used these technological tools in the past is not important here—what is important is that the potential online instructor has enough of a technological background to operate an LMS effectively and an interest to learn new technologies that can deliver online education effectively and efficiently. I can tell you from personal experience that I have learned to use a good deal of online education technological tools and I look forward to learning how to use many more of them.

I AM READY TO START—WHERE DO I TEACH?

Now that you have completed your self-assessment and are ready to teach online, where do you teach? As mentioned in the book's introduction, you can find online education in most educational fields, including secondary education (such as K12.us), but this book will focus on post-secondary education.

My first experience with choosing a school to teach in was really made for me—a recruiter reviewed my resume (most likely having seen it online from an employment website dealing with educational backgrounds), contacted me, and started me with an introduction to online teaching. Having found it very compatible and enjoyable after teaching one term, I continued teaching for this school to the present. Looking back, however, I was very lucky to have found a school that met and matched my needs to successfully teach online. Intuition and risk-taking are good personal traits to have, but if I had to redo my online education career, I would most likely have conducted some research to determine if the school met my needs professionally, and if I believed that I would be a good and valued addition to the school (and vice versa).

What, then, are some factors that determine if a school is a good fit for online teaching? Here are some considering factors:

- **School accreditation**
  Most post-secondary schools have accreditation standards in place to ensure that their academic programs meet compliance with their expectations and outcomes; in other words, that students successfully learn and apply the knowledge that they learn from attending classes, taking examinations, and writing papers. A regulatory body, such as a state department of education, or the US Department of Education, can close a school if they are not compliant with accreditation.
- **Class size**
  Is the average class size not too large (or not too small) to encourage effective learning and teaching?
- **Professional development**
  Does a school provide its own professional development programs to ensure that online instructors remain current with educational trends, as well as their own fields of study?

- **Technology**
  Is the technology that a school uses to teach its classes (such as an online learning platform, like Moodle or Blackboard), current and updated regularly? Is there a well-managed IT help desk to assist both online instructors and students?

WHERE DO I FIND A SCHOOL AND HOW DO I BEGIN THE APPLICATION PROCESS?

As I had mentioned earlier, a recruiter from a post-secondary school had called me to find out if I was interested in teaching online (most likely, having reviewed my resume online), and, thanks to a bit of luck and determination (and a self-assessment described in this chapter), I began work as an online instructor. However, this may or may not occur for many potential online instructors; they will need to conduct some initial research to find a school and an academic program that is a good match for them.

The beginning part of conducting research consists of determining which schools and programs match your academic background and skills; a prospective online instructor can review school rankings or accreditation rankings and data (much of this can be found online) to make a determination. Of course, not every potential business management instructor will begin their online careers at the Harvard University Business School, but there are a good deal of reputable and worthwhile academic programs (both for-profit and not-for-profit) that a candidate should not rule out.

The easiest method to apply for online instructor positions is to search for them on the school's employment website or through an employment website, such as Careerbuilder.com. But there are other nontraditional methods to finding online instructor employment. This can be as simple as contacting a dean at a prospective school to schedule an appointment to discuss employment or attending an open house or a networking event sponsored by the school. Of course, your application will have to proceed through formal channels, but attending these networking events or scheduling an appointment can help you learn more about the school in a professional, yet informal, setting.

In addition to determining an appropriate academic program, a prospective online instructor should ask questions about the students—what are their academic backgrounds, what prerequisite coursework do they need before they begin their academic program, what academic support do they receive. You can speak to a dean to answer these (and many other) questions; another good idea is to research the school's academic catalog (usually available to the public online at the school's website), or to attend a school's open house as a prospective student. This may sound like a far-fetched idea, but attending an open house event as a would-be student allows a prospective online instructor to truly determine what academic programs a school offers to its prospective students, and how a school successfully educates its student body. Attending such an event may answer more questions than a formal meeting with an academic dean.

With a bit of research and foresight, a prospective online instructor can determine which online schools are the best schools to begin their teaching careers. In the next chapter, I will discuss time management skills and strategies for potential online instructors.

CHAPTER 3

Time Management for Online Instructors

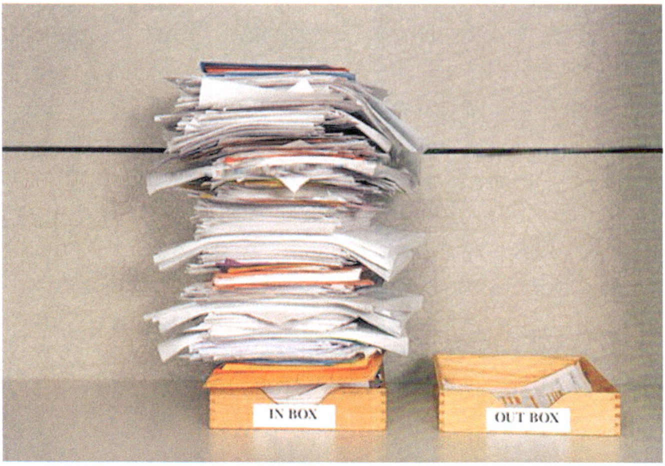

The Art of Teaching Online. DOI: http://dx.doi.org/10.1016/B978-0-08-101013-6.00003-5

In my first book, *Managing the One-Person Library*, I wrote a chapter dealing with time management for solo librarians, or librarians who manage their libraries on their own with minimal additional staff. Time management skills, of course, need to be an integral part of any professional's schedule, and this is especially true of online instructors. Most online instructors, as mentioned in earlier chapters of this book, work full-time for another company or organization, or work at different jobs, necessitating good time management skills needed to successfully teach online courses. There are numerous books and courses that promise the benefits of good time management skills, but I have found that most professionals interested in teaching online courses already possess these skills, or they would not consider a career in online education (or, could also just skip this chapter for the next one!) Nevertheless, a successful professional may possess these skills, but learning never ends, and sharpening these skills (through their other work or just learning a new skill or two by attending a webinar or reading an article) will ensure that any future online instructor will be able to balance their other career with an additional teaching career. For those individuals who do need more information on how to improve their time management skills, this chapter will assist them in organizing their time effectively and efficiently.

TIME MANAGEMENT SKILLS IN A NUTSHELL

Some professionals may find time management to be confining and restrictive; they believe that they do not need to create a schedule covering every possible minute of their workday in order to feel fully organized and busy at all times. But time management does not have to be so all-encompassing; potential online instructors should think of it as a skeleton to embellish later with bones, muscles, blood, and organs. It should be seen as a first step in organizing their daily schedules.

Time management can be summed up as follows:

- Time management allows professionals to accomplish their daily tasks effectively and efficiently.
- Time management plans should be flexible to allow for any changes in a professional's schedule.
- Time management plans should allow professionals to deal with their customers first.
- Time management plans should vary daily to allow for changes in a professional's tasks.
- Each and every day, create a to-do list and prioritize that list with the most important task that needs to be completed on that day. Then prioritize other daily tasks in the order you think those tasks need to be handled. Always remember to check off a task when you have finished it—this may sound trivial, but I have found that checking off a finished task gives an enormous sense of accomplishment and spurs me on to complete the next task.
- Break your larger tasks into smaller, more doable tasks that can be completed on a daily basis—this "chunking" makes an insurmountable task or project much easier to deal with (and keeps the hair on your head intact!). Small changes, such as chunking or checking off completed tasks, can give a solo librarian the confidence to organize and complete daily tasks and larger projects.

USEFUL ONLINE INSTRUCTOR TIME MANAGEMENT APPS

Much of these skills a professional can accomplish with paper, pen, and a calendar or any organizer. However, most of the world owns a smartphone, and the availability of time management apps available to any professional has allowed for more effective time management skills, inasmuch as documents and the ability to manage, organize, and send them is found in one location that fits in the palm of a hand—truly an amazing occurrence. Many professionals, however, do use the time-honored, old-fashioned paper, pen, and weekly or monthly organizer. Count me as one of those professionals; for many years, I did not see the need (or the desire) to own a smartphone, as I did not know what I would use it for (beyond the games, social media, and selfies that I don't use). Nevertheless, many professionals do use their smartphones to manage and to organize their time successfully.

I can say now (with humility) that I will be soon be the proud owner of a smartphone, as my contract on my old flip phone expires shortly. So I have been using my wife's older smartphone (still running on 4G) and have been impressed by the number and usefulness of the many apps available to smartphone owners, especially those that will help professionals manage their time efficiently and effectively. What apps have I discovered and used and what would work best for me?

The primary caveat here, of course, is that what I find favorable and useful in an app, another professional may not—one man's meat is another man's poison, to use the old saying.

I could write an entire book about time management apps; the conventional wisdom always says there is an app for every work task. The purpose of these apps is to organize a professional's time, and there are apps for every type of organization. I would suggest brainstorming and determining what you need to organize and how you will do it—this will determine for you what apps are most helpful and beneficial to your time organization.

I now describe two time management smartphone apps and explain why I find them useful and beneficial—**Dropbox** (https://www.dropbox.com/) and **Universal Password Manager** (http://upm.sourceforge.net/).

I use Dropbox on my desktop computer when I work from home, but I have used the app on my smartphone as well, and I have discovered how wonderful and convenient it is to be able to open and to move documents from my desktop's hard drive to my smartphone. This allows me to work on writing articles or my book anywhere I have Wi-Fi access, so if I have some free time, I can write anywhere.

As I grow older, I forget my passwords, and I have too many of them to remember just by using my memory. The Universal Password Manager (UPM) allows for storage of passwords, usernames, URLs, and simple memoranda in an encrypted database, all protected by only one password. A UPM can run on most operating systems (including Mac), as well as allow for database syncing across desktops and other devices (via a Dropbox account—another good reason to use Dropbox!) Not having to remember every password for every account is truly a time saver.

From my ongoing research on time management apps for smartphones, I discovered that the most useful apps provide the most time saved and organized successfully, as well being easy to set up and use. Perhaps my foray into using a smartphone may convert some potential online instructors standing on the edge of smartphone use, wanting to take the plunge. I say, come on in—the water is fine.

To conclude, time management for online instructors is really not very different than for any other professionals; it is a self-paced, self-taught learning skill that usually occurs at their primary job to ensure that they complete their tasks in a timely and organized manner. The key to good time management skills is to never stop learning, to add new skills, and to discard skills that may not work as they had in the past (pen, paper, and calendars come to mind here.) With an open and an inquisitive mind, a potential online instructor can make good use of their time and serve their students successfully.

CHAPTER 4

Professional Development

The Art of Teaching Online. DOI: http://dx.doi.org/10.1016/B978-0-08-101013-6.00004-7

A key area of maintaining self-education and knowledge of new material for anyone in any occupation or field is with professional development. And this is especially important in the area of online education, as many accredited schools require their online instructors to maintain their professional development status on a regular basis (e.g., quarterly) to ensure that the instructors remain knowledgeable in their chosen fields (as well as in educational subjects). This accreditation requirement ensures a competent and knowledgeable faculty, but many instructors forget how important professional development is to remain current in their fields and to ensure enhanced teaching skills. I am fortunate that my school, at the end of each quarter (with the exception of the fall quarter, since the quarter ends around Christmas) provides online webinars as part of our professional development. These webinars cover a vast array of educational subjects, so that online instructors only need to find webinars or other educational material related to their field of knowledge on their own. But what if an instructor's school does not offer professional development as my school does? What are the ways to accomplish a richer and more varied professional development? I will describe several below.

MEETINGS AND NETWORKING

Meetings are a time-honored method of networking and learning from other professionals in an online instructor's field; there is something positive to be said for meeting other professionals face-to-face and learning about new trends and issues in a person's field of work. It also helps to leave an office for a while and converse with peers in a relaxed and open setting. The explosive growth of online education has also created many online meetings and conferences that occur throughout the year; the Online Learning Consortium hosts several educational conferences throughout the year. However, many professionals cannot leave their jobs to take advantage of networking opportunities, or may not have the budgets available to attend meetings and conferences. However, many conferences, including the Online Learning Consortium's conferences, offer a virtual option to attend live or archived sessions at the professional's own pace or schedule. A new idea that has been developed among librarians (but can also apply to many professionals) in the last few years is the Personal Learning Network, or PLN, which can also serve as a professional development model for most professionals. According to Nelson (2012), "a PLN can be defined simply as a group of people who interact for the purpose of learning, and who give and take with the goal of sharing, growing, and being an active participant for a greater cause." A PLN, then, is an informal meeting of professionals. For professionals, given smartphones, Skype, and the Internet, a PLN is precisely what they need to network and to meet other professionals to share information and experiences in their given fields.

WEBINARS AND PODCASTS

Technological advances in the last decade alone have allowed for meetings to be held online—many organizations offer free (or limited cost) webinars on a vast variety of topics so that professionals can stay current and up-to-date with all sorts of trends and issues in their chosen fields. Professional consortia and organizations offer a good deal of webinars and podcasts to their members. Podcasting of webinars and other educational events offers even more flexibility for professionals to learn at home, away from work on their own schedules. In addition to the ubiquitous YouTube, podcasts can be found on most professional association sites, as well as on many commercial websites.

Many professionals, however, do proclaim the superiority of live events—you are meeting the person, listening to a live lecture, and asking questions to the presenter. This may lose something in a webinar setting, but with the exception of not being present at the lecture, a professional can participate in a webinar and ask questions the same as their live-attending counterparts. Webinars and podcasts can also save on travel costs and reduce the time a professional is away from their work, further proving their value as a training and development tool. Webinars and podcasts are an enhancement of the live lecture, and while they will never replace the live lecture, they are a useful and resourceful addition to an online instructor's professional development, given their limitations on time and budget.

SOCIAL MEDIA AND NETWORKING

In addition to numerous webinars and podcasts available for professional development, online instructors can network and make new professional connections via social media; Twitter, Facebook, and LinkedIn are the main social media sites that are being used by numerous professionals to contact other professionals and learn from them or work with them on projects or other aspects of their work. Of these sites, LinkedIn is perhaps the most useful, as professionals can chat with similar professionals, post their resume, search for additional projects to work on with other professionals, and just receive help and assistance with questions that they may have. Twitter and Facebook are also very good for just communicating with a vast number of professional contacts (Twitter, of course, with its 140 character limit, does not have the advantages of posting material and conversing over a long period of time as Facebook does, but Twitter is useful for professional development announcements or updates), which makes them good sites for this task. Listservs are another convenient and easy way to make contacts with other online instructors in their fields, learn about various conferences and webinars available, and find out about the latest trends, technologies, and strategies available to them. One caveat here should be mentioned about social media and networking—online instructors should only post, of course, professional information and the information that they wish others to see and to read, and should become aware of the terms and conditions of each of the social media sites that they choose to utilize for their professional development (terms and conditions documents are very lengthy, but should be reviewed, as they deal with posted content and who owns that content, for instance.) Terms of Service Didn't Read (www.tosdr.org) is an excellent website that provides concise summaries of the main social media web sites, such as Twitter and Facebook, that can help an online instructor navigate these important terms and decide which social media website works best for their needs.

WRITING

While not all online instructors will want (or need) to write a book on their experiences, many of them can gain visibility in their professional community by offering to write book or Internet reviews for the vast number of library publications. In the past 10 years, I have written Internet and book reviews for *Library Journal, School Library Journal, Reference and Users Quarterly*, and *College & Research Library News*. Writing these reviews allows an online instructor to sharpen their writing skills that will help them as they prepare their coursework, as well as maintain a visibility in their professional communities. The more ambitious professionals can also volunteer to help other professionals to write a peer-reviewed article on a topic that interests them or that they have knowledge in researching and writing. Doing so also contributes to learning and improving one's writing skills, as well as increasing and enhancing the visibility of their organizations where they work, as is the case not only with an online instructor's writing scholarly articles and books, but also in collaborating with their fellow professionals in writing scholarly articles.

Those professionals who want to become successful online instructors will need to continually burnish and hone their professional development skills, in order to ensure that their teaching and knowledge skills remain current and exemplary. Learning truly never ends, whether the learning takes place among students or among teachers.

CHAPTER 5

Incorporating the Human Factor in Online Instruction, Part 1

The Art of Teaching Online. DOI: http://dx.doi.org/10.1016/B978-0-08-101013-6.00005-9

This chapter will discuss what is the most important issue in online education and instruction, the importance and necessity of creating a human presence in an online environment so that students will successfully learn skills that will allow them to complete their degree work and begin a career in their chosen field. As I have said in the introduction to this book, I understand that online instruction will not supplant live instruction, given live instruction's ability to create and to foster a personal, one-on-one interaction with an instructor, but given the need for education programs that can be made available to all for a reasonable price, online instruction will become an important and prominent presence in education alongside traditional education. And this is also true for nondegree educational programs, such as continuing education, where webinars and other educational programs will allow professionals the ability to enroll in programs at their own pace and timing, in order to meet continuing education accreditation requirements for their career fields.

I will say at the outset that online instruction is not for everyone; many instructors (as well as students) do not like or approve of solely electronic interaction between instructor and student. They want and require the face-to-face, personal interaction between student and instructor that has been the feature of most education since the days of Socrates and Aristotle. Students may also not want self-paced courses at the outset of their education, and wish to be guided with more frequency by a live instructor. There is nothing wrong with these desires; it is an integral part of human life and society to interact with other people. But given many students' busy work schedules, family life, and other commitments (as well as students returning to school later in life), the traditional method of education does not fit their needs to complete their educational programs. Online instruction allows them to learn anywhere and anytime; however, online students need to be more organized than their traditional education counterparts, since online instruction does not (usually) require attendance in class. Online students must be able to manage their time and prioritize their work more successfully than their traditional education counterparts. Therefore, the successful online instructor not only imparts knowledge and education, but facilitates knowledge and education; they need to ensure that students complete their work successfully, but within an online environment, which is not always easy. Yet technology today allows for a wide and large degree of personal contact comparable to face-to-face interaction. Before I write further, I would like potential online instructors to perform an emotional self-assessment to ensure that online instruction, versus traditional instruction, is the proper mode of instruction for them.

An important self-assessment for a potential online instructor is to assess their emotional intelligence (EQ). Emotional intelligence is similar to the measure of intelligence quotient (or IQ) in that EQ measures a person's emotional level and ability to deal with and to overcome issues that can appear on a daily basis (as well as over a period of time). The author Daniel Goleman (2005) coined this term "emotional intelligence" within the last 20 years, and wrote a book on this topic with the same name, focusing on how the main traits of emotional intelligence (empathy, self-control, and self-motivation) are important for building strong, positive, and lasting relationships, both at work and in one's personal life. There have been several recent studies dealing with emotional intelligence as an important determinant for success in online learning (Berenson et al., 2008; Buzdar et al., 2016), but to my knowledge, few studies have been published that deal with emotional intelligence and the ability to become a successful online instructor. Nevertheless, my experience over the last several years as an online instructor, I can state very comfortably and positively that the higher (or better) a professional's emotional intelligence measures, the more successful (and happy) those professionals will become as online instructors (not to mention the importance of successfully facilitating and teaching their students online). What emotional intelligence means with regard to online instruction is not the breadth of knowledge that a potential online instructor possesses, but the emotional knowledge a potential online instructor possesses. This is the ability to empathize with their students' ability to succeed in their classes. This is not an easy feat, as online students, especially those in classes with shorter times (half a semester versus a whole semester, for instance) are pressed to not only successfully learn and demonstrate their learning of the material, but also learn to organize their time successfully to accomplish the above goals. The potential online instructor with good emotional intelligence skills will successfully assist their students to meet their goals, with exemplary facilitation skills that complement their emotional intelligence characteristics.

What are these facilitation skills? They are a combination of an online instructor's subject knowledge as well as their level of emotional intelligence. I had mentioned earlier about a potential instructor's empathy, which I believe to be the key to exemplary online instruction. Empathy is the ability to emotionally put yourself in your students' place—what would you do to help them or to assist them in succeeding in their coursework, for instance? By assistance, I do not mean giving the students the answers or to complete their work for them; using empathy selectively and carefully, a successful online instructor creates a rapport with the students and allows them to become comfortable in asking the instructor for help and guidance. Creating a good rapport with online students can be as simple as being available for them not just during specific weekly office hours, but also during most of the day (an online instructor, of course, should limit availability during evenings or during the middle of the night!) The presence and proliferation of email, instant messaging, and texting makes being available for students and responding to their questions easier and faster than holding set office hours. The greater an instructor's empathy towards their students, the more available they will be to respond to their students' needs. However, a good online instructor needs to set limits on empathy and not have their students take advantage of their concern and desire to help by ignoring their instructor's help until the last minute before an assignment due date, or by criticizing them for a grade that they feel they did not deserve. Good emotional intelligence skills enable an online instructor to know when to be fair and when to be firm with students, whether they are college-age or adults returning to school after a long period of time. Good emotional intelligence skills also allow an online instructor the proper motivation to not only learn more about their own subject knowledge, but also to learn how to help their students more in areas not familiar to instructors, such as with troubleshooting technology. My school has a wonderful and helpful computer support desk available 24 hours a day, 7 days a week, but I do try to keep my computer troubleshooting skills sharp and fresh in order for my students to have quick access to my knowledge and not to have to wait for assistance from a help desk (which may take a long time). Employing good emotional intelligence and empathy skills allows for an online instructor to be proactive, helpful, and understanding to their students, ensuring that their education is a useful, practical, and worthwhile experience.

CHAPTER 6

Incorporating the Human Factor in Online Instruction, Part 2

From my experience as an online instructor, the biggest obstacle online students face is fear—fear that they will not understand the material in a class, fear that they will fall behind with their assignments, and (most of all) fear of failing a course and then having to reenroll in the

The Art of Teaching Online. DOI: http://dx.doi.org/10.1016/B978-0-08-101013-6.00006-0

course (a big fear, considering that most students borrow money to pay for their tuition). The best way to allay a student's fears is to listen to them and to offer advice, but most importantly, to respond to their concerns (whether by telephone, e-mail message, or text messaging) as quickly as possible. A good yardstick of response time is either overnight, or no more than 24 hours, but the faster the response, the more effective your assistance will be to your students. I can tell you that my one obsession is checking my email messages too often for my own good, but I passionately believe that if a student needs help, they need to be helped as quickly as possible. I cannot tell you how wonderful it is to receive acknowledgment from my students that I could assist them. It reminds me of one of my colleagues, who once suggested writing the words "thank you" in response to a student's message to acknowledge receipt of an assignment or just to answer a question. She said that it can make all the difference in the world to a student who needs assistance that someone listens to them and to their concerns.

Now no instructor is all-knowing; what if an online instructor cannot directly answer a student's question? The next step would be to direct the student to a campus dean, campus director, or another instructor who can assist them and answer their questions correctly. Many years of managing libraries has made me an expert in the art of referrals to the proper people who can help questioning patrons and students; it is an integral part of my job and it is not a bother to me to do this (even though many patrons and students apologize when they ask me a question! I immediately put them at ease by telling them that the only stupid question is the one you do not ask.) And that is the first step in using empathy to your advantage as an online instructor—put the student at ease, and let them know that their concerns are your concerns. What is the next step? Not every online instructor is, of course, a reference librarian, but every online instructor can become very knowledgeable in their field, as well as become very knowledgeable about their school's policies, troubleshooting personal computers, and any other aspects of their school's academic policies. Forewarned and forearmed, as Cervantes once said.

It is one aspect of emotional intelligence to be able to understand and to empathize with students who may be ill at ease, nervous, or new to online education to ally their fears—what about students who do not complete their assignments and do not participate in the online classroom? With my online courses, attendance usually consists of the number of times a student will log in to the course (and the frequency of duration). It is a good idea if your learning information management system (LIMS), or online course platform, contains the number of times and frequency a student logs in to the course; this is an indication of the student's active participation in the course, so if you don't see current login activity from a student, you need to contact the student, as well as contact the student's dean. The question here is what mode of communication to use—do you send an email message or do you contact the student by telephone? My opinion on this is that either is a good option, but I would prefer the telephone, as having direct, vocal contact may make the student feel more at ease, and, more importantly, feel as if someone cares to go the extra mile to ensure that the student should (and, hopefully, will) take their education seriously. As an instructor, you may leave a good deal of messages on an answering machine, and a student may just pay lip service to what you have to say and to do, but I will tell you that one time, I had a student falling behind in her work, and I called her to find out why this occurred. She was so upset about being behind in her work that she cried during our conversation. I immediately put her at ease, told her that I wanted her to succeed in the course, and set up a schedule for her to submit her assignments to receive credit for them. Remember that a voice is more persuasive, helpful, and useful than an e-mail message.

The next question arises—how do you handle problem students? Not the students that don't complete their assignments; I am referring to ones that exhibit bad behavior in the course, whether it is improper language in a discussion forum, or rudeness to an online instructor. The first part of the solution is to defuse what can be a tense situation for both the instructor and the student—the instructor must be the adult in such a situation, and must remain calm during the student's venting about what is troubling him or her. The instructor, after a short interval, should gently calm the student down and tell the student that the instructor would be happy to help them if they can talk calmly and rationally to the instructor. This usually allows the student to calm down and work with the instructor to solve the problem. This situation can occur either on a telephone or online via email or instant message or texts. It is harder to discern a student's tone and behavior in written form, but it can be done with a bit of practice and common sense. I once had a student who sent me an email message about his dissatisfaction with his assignment's grade; I could read by his message that he was a bit rude and sarcastic in his tone to me. I told him that I gave him the grade he deserved and that he needed to respect me as an instructor more than in his current state. He stopped and apologized for his behavior (perhaps he was angry about another issue in his life and he took his anger out on me.) We had a very good and productive relationship for the remainder of the course—maintaining a calm attitude, along with ensuring that the instructor is in charge of the situation, goes a long way towards creating a positive working relationship with your students.

There is an art and a science to successful online instruction; while online instruction can be measured and quantified as the science aspect, I believe the more important aspect of successful online instruction is the art; empathy, emotional intelligence, and common sense are the real qualities of a successful online instructor and can truly only be cultivated with trial and error. Keeping an open mind, as well trying and experimenting with new ideas or strategies to improve the human aspect of online education, is the hallmark of a successful online instructor.

CHAPTER 7

Strategies to Teach Online Students Successfully

The Art of Teaching Online. DOI: http://dx.doi.org/10.1016/B978-0-08-101013-6.00007-2

Many books dealing with online education focus on pedagogy, which, according to Webster's Collegiate Dictionary, is "the art, science, or profession of teaching." (Merriam-Webster, 1986). This book focuses on the art of teaching rather than the science of teaching (and since most of you reading this book wish to enter the online teaching profession, I will not focus on this area either.). Online education attracts a good deal of adult learners as well as college-age learners; in fact, from my years as an online instructor, I would say that more students are adult learners who are returning to school, either not having pursued a postsecondary education before or having started their education but are now returning to school to complete their education. Why are they returning? These students, having completed their academic degree, will find better employment with these educational credentials. Their companies require that they complete their education in order to remain with the company as an employee. So most adult, or returning, students (no matter what age) possess the motivation, or desire, to begin, to continue, and to complete their education. This is a very laudable goal, and most students do complete their education successfully. But some students, even those with the best of intentions and motivation, do not successfully complete their online education, and either lose or do not advance in their work and in their profession. The goal of the successful online instructor is to ensure that all of his or her students succeed in their education, but it is a two-way street to ensure success, as students and instructors need to teach each other how to learn successfully. This chapter deals with the art of motivating students properly so that they succeed in their education, and how to deal with students who may not be motivated enough to succeed in finishing their courses. Accomplished online instructors teach their course material to their students successfully, but also facilitate proper learning by ensuring that all students participate in the learning process to their fullest capability, whether they wish to do so or do not wish to do so. The challenge in the successful art of online instruction is to motivate the unmotivated.

Adult, or returning, students (from my experience) fall into two categories—those who are excited to learn and willing to learn, and those who are just there for the ride, so to speak. They require the degree to either continue with their employment or to advance their employment, and even this crucial inducement does not motivate them to learn new skills. And this goal, the learning and application of new skills, is what I stress in my teaching, whether it is in the feedback I include in my student's assignments, or in the live lectures I conduct. Nothing is as important in any education as the accumulation of skills that are necessary to advance their careers. This is the ideal motivator for many online students, but not all online students. Many online students also work full time, and do not have the ability or the luxury of being able to attend classes full time to devote to their studies, and many online students fall behind in their coursework due to their working full time (or many online students use the excuse of having to work full time to not complete their coursework either on time or at all). Finally, an online instructor may find students who have been coerced or pushed into an education program by parents, spouses, or friends against their will or best wishes, and do not want to learn or to complete their education.

What strategies should the successful online instructor use to motivate students and to deal with stubborn or reluctant learners? There are many pedagogical books available that discuss different types of learners and what skills they possess (or do not possess), and how an online instructor can understand and motivate these learners. These books are useful as references, but this book deals with a perspective from an experienced online instructor, and what I have seen and applied to ensure that my students succeed in their coursework.

The first, and I believe the most effective, motivation strategy is to maintain a constant presence online. The most successful online instructors not only give proper and detailed feedback of their students' assignments and coursework, but log in regularly (by this I mean several times a day) to answer email questions and to just show students (who may be online at the same time) that their instructor is there and is a constant presence online. This also extends to grading assignments as quickly as possible and answering email messages as possible (however, many schools have requirements regarding proper deadlines for these tasks.) The key for the successful online instructor is to go *above and beyond* these requirements to connect with these students; this is crucial in an online environment where personal contact is very minimal. Maintaining this constant presence, like many educational strategies, is not a perfect strategy, but I have found it does make a difference between a motivated student and an unmotivated student—I cannot tell you how satisfied I feel when a student has told me that my maintaining constant contact with them has helped them succeed in my course. Maintaining constant contact may require going out of an online instructor's comfort zone—for instance, instant messaging or using Skype to respond faster to students (as opposed to an email message or a voicemail message) may seem too intrusive for some instructors, but if online students use these technologies to communicate to each other, online instructors need to use them too, in order to maintain as much of a constant online presence as possible.

And this is a good introduction to the importance of the successful online instructor's use of technology to motivate students in their coursework. My school requires that I conduct a live weekly lecture for my students. For a course without much personal contact, a live, weekly lecture, by delivering educational material via a webcam, is a powerful motivator for students. To see and hear who teaches them makes them want to succeed in their course—they see a presence there and want to learn. If your school does not use an online lecture platform (such as Adobe Connect or WebEx) to hold live lectures, there are other technologies available, such as GoToMeeting. Your school, like mine, may require a weekly live online lecture as part of your instructional duties, but I strongly suggest that you provide weekly lectures for your online students if they are not required—not only do your students connect with you and become motivated, but you learn new speaking skills (to present your lectures), content skills (to write your lectures), and new technological skills (to operate your lectures).

Finally, empathy, as we have seen in an earlier chapter, is a powerful motivational tool for online students. An online instructor need not have enrolled in an online course to feel empathy for their students; a successful online instructor has the cognitive and emotional skills to listen to students (whether talking on the telephone or Skype, sending an instant message, or writing an email message) and understand what they are going through. A resourceful instructor will be able to provide websites or other information students would need to successfully complete their assignments, and can engage in an informal conversation with students (within proper professional boundaries, of course) to demonstrate to them that their instructor wants them to succeed in their coursework.

Most online students are already motivated to succeed in their classes, and many more can be motivated with these strategies, as well as the successful online instructor's skills. But what about stubborn online students or reluctant online learners who cannot be reached by these skills and strategies? It is important and imperative for the successful online instructor to have the patience to continue to try to help these students, but here it is also crucial to maintain a good relationship with your campus dean. The dean has the ability to discipline a student in different ways than an online instructor does, but it should be stressed that the online instructor should make the most effort to help these students.

There is a science to instruction, as the word *pedagogy* states, but from my experience, successful online instruction is primarily an art. Through instructors' knowledge, as well as plain common sense, they can provide the best possible educational experience for their online students.

REFERENCE

Merriam-Webster, Inc. (1986). *Merriam-Webster's Ninth New Collegiate Dictionary*. Springfield, MA: Merriam-Webster, Inc., Publishers.

CHAPTER 8

Online Faculty Provide Insights Into Successful Online Instruction

INTRODUCTION

A book about online education would be deficient if I did not include several interviews from a current online faculty. This chapter will include questions and answers from an instructor at an Associate's, Bachelor's, and Master's degree-granting institution that primarily offers online courses, where I have worked as an online instructor since 2011. The next section will include questions and answers about online education from a Northern Arizona University faculty.

Michelle Miller, PhD

Dr. Michelle Miller is a professor of psychology at Northern Arizona University. She earned her Ph.D. in cognitive psychology from UCLA.

Dr. Miller's research focuses on language and memory. Specifically, she has studied how normal aging affects the ability to produce and comprehend language, language production in brain-injured individuals, and how people produce and comprehend descriptions of interpersonal violence, such as crime reports published in mass media.

Dr. Miller also has interests in applied cognitive psychology, particularly how different pedagogical strategies affect student comprehension and retention of material in the social and natural sciences.

Dr. Miller was honored to become one of NAU's President's Distinguished Teaching Fellows in 2011.

She is the author of *Minds Online: Teaching Effectively With Technology*, published by Harvard University Press in 2014.

Larry MacPhee

Larry MacPhee is an Associate Director at the e-Learning Center and was the director of Northern Arizona University's Center for

The Art of Teaching Online. DOI: http://dx.doi.org/10.1016/B978-0-08-101013-6.00008-4

Technology Enhanced Learning from 2001 until its merger with the e-Learning Center in 2006. He has a background in science research and education, has a Master's Degree in Biology, and has been promoting creative instructional uses of technology since the early days of personal computing. His professional interests include thinking and speaking about technology trends, technical writing, usability and interface design, web design, computer troubleshooting, learning space design, and science and technology instruction. He currently teaches Bio 100 L, a fully online, hands-on, laboratory science class.

1. *Please summarize what pedagogical skills new online instructors should have and how they can develop these skills.*
   Miller:
   - They need to have excellent written communication skills, meaning that they write in a way that is not just clear and comprehensible, but also courteous and inviting. Instructors can practice writing welcome emails to students, for example, or passages within the syllabus, that achieve the kind of tone and clarity that they want, and then get feedback from colleagues or former students to fine-tune their work.
   - They need to be able to explain to students what's expected in online discussion and be able to keep the discussion going while preventing potential conflict or incivility among discussants. Exploring and participating in different nonacademic discussion communities (e.g., Reddit, Ravelry) can be a way to practice these skills and learn how online discussions work. This is also an excellent opportunity to see how *not* to communicate online, and just how spectacularly things can—and do—go wrong when people engage with each other online.
   - They need to have creative ideas about how to present, explain and reinforce course material that goes beyond just pages of text, slideshows, or links to TED talks. Professional development, working with instructional designers, and looking at other web courses for inspiration are good sources for these ideas.
2. *What strategies and techniques (pedagogical and technological) do you use to enhance the human aspect of online education?*
   Miller: It's hard to say for sure which techniques motivated students the most, but I have used a combination of the following:
   - Emphasizing the sense of discovery, shared mission and community in a course. For example, students are explicitly asked in

some discussion assignments to offer supportive statements to one another.
- Incremental, small-stakes assignments that are rapidly graded and returned and make it clear how quickly students are progressing through the course.
- Asking students to relate material to their lives, apply course concepts to their lives, or tell personal stories (within appropriate limits).
- Emphasizing novelty and unexpected connections in the material and concepts.
- Use of an upbeat, optimistic tone in communications.

MacPhee: Try to make the class engaging, with use of media, current events, interesting, and fun assignments which may involve real-world activities rather than online work, and encourage student interaction, by way of group work or presentations. Provide regular deadlines to prevent students from letting work pile up, but also be forgiving, within reason, of late work, since most online students are balancing their personal and work life with their studies. Provide timely feedback to make sure students know their work is being recognized. Avoid assignments with answers that can be easily "Googled" and focus instead on how they would solve a problem by giving them a scenario, or asking them to justify their opinion on how they would respond to an ethical dilemma, for example. Assign more low-stakes assignments with lower point values, rather than high-point comprehensive exams when possible. Make use of machine gradable assessments as checks on progress, but also assign work that involves some writing, research, or critical thinking. Allow them to use the tools they have at hand, such as Google, since it's hard to stop them. Make the assignments more about the synthesis of information rather than the recall of facts.

3. *How do you deal with at-risk students to ensure their academic success?*
Miller: In my opening discussion posts and other communications, I invite (but don't require) students to disclose issues that might affect their performance in class, or what they would like me to know about them. Acknowledging these challenges early on, and personally affirming to the student that I believe that they can—and will—succeed, seems to help students get off to a good start. I email students whose first log-ins are late or infrequent, to ask if everything is okay and to remind them of the course expectations. Lastly, I offer a range of types of assignments to maximize the chances that students will

find some kind of work in which they can excel. I also have policies that allow late work within limits, such as one free 48-hour extension that they can use with no questions asked.

4. *What do you believe are the most positive factors of online education? The most negative ones?*

   MacPhee: The most positive aspect of online education is that it removes many of the barriers of time and place from learning activities. A student who is working a day job, or can't attend class because she has a baby at home, can further their education by doing the work on a nontraditional schedule, and students who are geographically isolated can still get an education without having to travel which might be difficult or impossible. We have troops who are stationed in remote regions who are taking online classes and who return from overseas with a degree, and people who live in remote rural areas far from a traditional college or university who can get an education that helps them improve their situation. These make the difficulties of learning online worth the effort. We have seen that traditional universities generally don't lose enrollment when they offer online programs. Instead, they grow enrollment by offering the opportunity of an education to people who couldn't attend in the traditional way.

   The negatives are clear. The technology, for some people, can get in the way of the learning. It can be impersonal and isolating. It can be harder to get motivated and stay focused, often because a student may be piling their studies on top of an otherwise busy life, rather than dropping everything else and being a full-time student.

5. *What are the characteristics of a successful online learner?*

   Miller: On the one hand, I don't think that today's students are all that different from how students have always been. They learn with the same brains that human beings have had for a very long time, and they face a lot of the same struggles that people have always encountered in the course of trying to learn more and become more than they are.

   The one big difference is that we now have the ambitious, and I think noble, goal of bringing higher learning to more people than ever before. Opportunities and information that would have once been reserved for a privileged few are now—at least in theory—thrown open for anyone who's willing to invest the effort. I think it's easy to forget just what a huge and breathtaking project this is. Seen in this light, why wouldn't we use every method at our disposal to accomplish the mission? This includes having some or all of one's higher education coming in the form of online courses.

MacPhee: Human beings, even introverts, are social creatures. We thrive on interaction with others. Replicating that valuable person-to-person interaction is possible in an online class, but it's challenging. We should strive to make an online course more of a community of learners and less of a correspondence course where communication is only between the individual and instructor. We can do this with group work, mediated by tools like Google Apps for Education, or wikis, where a group of learners is challenged to work together to create a report or, better yet, a presentation to the class. Making it fair is always a challenge with group work, but it can be effectively accomplished by using peer evaluation as part of the assessment process. When students know that they are accountable to their coworkers, they generally step up and accept the responsibility, because they know that their peers have a good sense of who did the work, and who made the biggest contributions to the group project.

The challenge to the online learner is isolation and, to a lesser degree, procrastination. In most online courses, the work is more self-paced than in a face-to-face class. A student in an online course has to motivate himself or herself to do the work, without the teacher hovering over their shoulder. In short, taking an online course requires motivation and self-discipline, because working in isolation without the regular reminders and encouragement can be demotivating. The instructor can help with these challenges by providing prompt feedback and assigning deadlines. Early intervention when a student is doing poorly, or is falling behind on assignments can be effective.

And the more pervasive online learning becomes, not just in higher education, but in other learning and professional situations, the more important it is that students acquire the ability *to* learn in that way. For example, a small business owner who wants to take advantage of all the resources available to them through, say, their local community college might find that those now involve online learning. And so, if they lack the skills or experience of learning in that way, they will be missing out. Professional development, professional certifications, public health resources—so many of these are going online that having done online learning in some form becomes an advantage in and of itself.

6. *What future do you see for online education?*

Miller: When I work with tech-oriented faculty and instructional designers, I'm always struck by how passionate they are about the promise of online learning to improve the lives of students, and really, to improve human life in general. A lot of smart people are working very hard—often behind the scenes, without much in the way of recognition or support—to realize this promise, and as long as those people's passion holds out I think we will continue to see this area improve and grow.

That said, I think we will also see some friction growing out of the gap between the idealistic promise of what we *could* do with online learning (and technologically aided education as a whole) and what we *actually* do. Constructing really good, really compelling online courses, ones that make the absolute most of what we can do with the technology, requires a massive investment of time and talent. I think given these costs, it's tempting to take shortcuts, whether with the content, the feedback students get, or the sophistication of the teaching tools, and so online courses do often fall short of what they could be. I think there will need to be closer communication between the faculty on the ground, administration, and the educational technology industry so that we can get better products made and faculty-supported in using those to build really great online courses. And similarly, I think we are finally at a point where schools are less likely to see online courses as a quick source of revenue, and students are less likely to see them as an easy A. This adjustment toward appropriate expectations is a good and necessary thing as online learning matures.

MacPhee: How can technology improve learning outcomes for online students?

I'm a fan of technology, but we need to be careful not to put the cart before the horse. Should we use Twitter (or other technologies) because it's new, trendy, or cool? Possibly, but why? Technology needs to serve the learning outcomes, and not the other way around. If we ask, "What are the learning outcomes?" and one of them is well-served by a particular technology, then we should adopt it. My concern is that, all too often, we pick a technology because it's trendy, and try to fit it to the instruction. This is forced, and usually turns out badly. A good technology should address a teaching and learning need. For example, let's say we're teaching a large class where we need feedback and engagement from all of the students, and we're only hearing from a small subset of vocal students who sit in the front row. That might be a good application for a live polling tool or, in an online class, an anonymous discussion board. This allows us to check the knowledge or opinions of a wider constituency. The pain of learning the technology is worth it, because the technology helps us to reach more of the students. Another good use of technology might be to bring in a guest lecturer via video conferencing (and chat for Q&A) who it would have been too expensive to bring to a class under normal circumstances. For example, maybe the students could talk to an astronaut on a space station, or a scientist in Antarctica, or a politician in Washington, DC, and have a chance to ask them questions after the presentation.

7. *MacPhee: What future technological trends do you see for online education?*
   Adaptive courseware tools, which uses algorithms to identify your level of mastery, and adjust the learning pathway accordingly, show promise. They can be used for readiness placement, for remedial work, and for asynchronous work so that learners can proceed at their own pace. Such tools should not, however, remove the human factor from the learning. It can be very demotivating to work hard and reach a milestone, only to be told, "Good job, [your name]!" by the computer, and then be given a new pile of harder work to complete, without any genuine recognition of what you have accomplished.

Lynne Croteau

Lynne Croteau is currently a Regional Dean, and has over 15 years of experience in higher education in operations and academics, both residentially and online. She participates in online learning and professional development with innovative teaching strategies and student engagement initiatives.

She also has over 20 years' management experience which includes working in education, training and development, sales, the healthcare industry, retail, and food service.

Her educational background consists of a Bachelor of Science in Business Management from Westfield State College in Westfield, Massachusetts; a Master of Human Resource Management (MHRM), and a Master of Business Administration (MBA), both from Keller Graduate School of Management of DeVry University.

1. *What is your professional background and when did you begin to teach online courses?*
   I am a full-time Academic Dean who teaches part-time. I have been in higher education in varied positions in academics, support, and

operations for about 17 years. I started teaching online 10 years ago in the business program (bachelor program).

2. *Why did you want to teach online?*
   There was an opportunity to teach online part-time, and I jumped on the opportunity. I was an online student when I completed my Master's degrees and enjoyed it.
3. *What courses have you taught online?*
   I have taught business courses (general and Human Resource Management-focused) which include the following:
   Introduction to Business, Principles of Management, Managing a Diverse Workforce, Employee Law, Introduction to Human Resource Management, Modern Human Resource Management, Contemporary Leadership Skills, Career Development, Strategic Staffing, Human Resource Capstone.
4. *What strategies and techniques (pedagogical and technological) do you use to enhance the human aspect of online education?*
   I look for opportunities to engage students as if it were a face-to-face environment using synchronous opportunities in WebEx, and sharing content in various learning styles. Having a differentiated instruction is important for our learners who prefer to learn in another method besides visual. I provide videos with audio, graphs and pictures, as well as scenarios related to real-world situations that the students may connect with in order to drive home the concepts.

   Making sure students are comfortable with reaching out to me is also important. I let the students know that they can reach me via phone, text, email or set up a WebEx session (WebEx is an online meeting platform somewhat similar to GoToMeeting.). I do, however, set parameters for instance, I answer do not calls or texts before 9:00 a.m. and after 9:00 p.m.
5. *How do you deal with at-risk students to ensure their academic success?*
   I reach out to all students who have missed their week one deadlines via email (course mail). If a student misses their second week deadlines as well as their first week, I call them. For the students that respond, I work with them as best I can to provide support. The best support that they appreciate is to have extra time to complete assignments with a reduced late penalty so, I typically oblige. I also work with the students one-on-one if needed (in my WebEx room).

6. *What do you believe are the most positive factors of online education? The most negative ones?*

   Positive:

   For both students and faculty:

   a. You have the flexibility to complete work at any time during the week (as long as it is done within the due dates).
   b. Online education allows students to enhance their writing skills for they are writing their discussions as well as assignments.

   Positive:

   For the faculty:

   a. We are perceived as being quite smart at times, for we have the ability to research and reply to any question that a student may ask us. If we were in the residential classroom setting and a student asked us a question that we did not know the answer to (off the top of our heads), we can only respond with "I'll get back to you on that." When asked the same question online, we can respond after researching and craft a brilliant response.
   b. There is no need to travel or to get dressed up for class.
   c. Can grade assignments as they come in (don't have to wait until a specific class time to collect them all on the same day).
      i. All assignments are digital (students don't pass in a paper that is a hardcopy). This helps with using plagiarism tools online.
   d. You can upload supplemental material into the class to help drive home the content (usually a YouTube video).
   e. You don't have to deal with the challenges of disruptive students.
   f. You tend to get feedback from students that may not open up in the residential classroom setting.
   g. If you teach the same course over and over, you can build a repository for all your supplemental work, discussion posts, grading rubrics, etc., in order to save time and to complete less work.

   Negative:

   For the faculty:

   a. The course can have constraints on content that is presented.
      i. For example, an assignment may not be an assignment that you feel is appropriate; however, you have to use it.

b. You tend to have more students enrolled in your course than you would have in a typically residential setting.
c. Deadlines for grading are usually less than a week.
d. Although you don't deal with the challenges of disruptive students, you may have a student that posts something inappropriate.
e. A feeling that you always need to be available and that you should be in your course every day.
f. If you teach a new class, there is a great deal of prep work to go into the course.

For the students:

a. Lack of time management skills is detrimental to their success.
b. If they have poor research and writing skills, they will not be successful.
c. Depending on how attentive the online instructor is, some students don't get the feedback they need on assignments or questions in time to complete current or future assignments.
d. Students may feel as if they are teaching themselves because they have to read everything instead of hearing the faculty member explain the content in a live classroom.

7. *What are the characteristics of a successful online learner?*
A successful online learner should have solid time management skills. Students that schedule time into their calendar as if the online course was a residential course are very successful. Also, students that go through the orientation on how to navigate through the online learning management system do well. Students who have the drive and motivation to succeed in their online courses are definitely successful online learners.
8. *How would you personally improve the quality of online education?*
   a. Provide training to faculty on:
      i. Learning Management System (how to navigate a course shell and how to use it successfully to teach).
      ii. How to build rubrics.
      iii. Focus on the content and not necessarily APA format.
      iv. How to set up a repository for future classes.
      v. How to use tools to help with differentiated learning.
      vi. YouTube.
      vii. Online teaching tools such as Animoto and Prezi.

   b. Build courses that use differentiated learning styles.
      i. Focus on authentic assessments.
      ii. Provide faculty with best practices for teaching the course in the faculty guide.
9. *What future do you see for online education?*
   a. Online education is here to stay the technology will be improved in order to have access on any smart device.
      i. Most likely more simulative technology for courses such as laboratories.
   b. Competency Based Education (based on prior knowledge that a student possesses) will be available, as well as faculty-led courses.
   c. Online education will become more of the norm for not only higher (postsecondary) education, but for secondary education as well.

Debra Bohlman

Debra Bohlman is currently a Chair in a General Education department; she has been a full-time faculty member at her college since 2000 and has also worked as a General Education Faculty Coordinator and as an Academic Dean. Her coursework has included Introduction to Literature, English Composition, Professional Communication, Reading and Writing Strategies, and Humanities.

1. *What is your professional background and when did you begin to teach online courses?*
   I have been teaching English classes at a college level for over 20 years and started teaching online in mid-2000.
2. *Why did you want to teach online?*
   I was interested in teaching online because it seemed like the new frontier of teaching and learning.
3. *What courses have you taught online?*
   I have taught English Composition, Humanities, Introduction to Critical Thinking, Creative Writing, and Introduction to Literature in online or blended courses.
4. *What strategies and techniques (pedagogical and technological) do you use to enhance the human aspect of online education?*
   To bring the human aspect to online teaching, I use some course features and different teaching techniques to help create an inviting and welcoming environment, to help create a genuine classroom

culture for students. First, on the home page, a photo with my contact information is at the upper right-hand corner for easy access. Second, I create an Open House tour video that is shared on the home page via the announcements and is sent to students in a welcome email. Third, through the announcements, I share teaching tips, guidance, article links, and create engagement by using tools such as Voki to share key course information to students. Fourth, in the weekly scheduled live lectures, I use a web cam because over half of the meaning of our words is communicated through facial expressions. By utilizing the camera, I am enhancing the human component and modeling effective and professional communication skills for students. I also let students know that their attendance in the live session is crucial for the whole class and that with their attendance something better and more inclusive is created, so we both need each other to create a valuable session. Also, in the lecture, key assignment details are shared and students are actively engaged throughout the session. Fifth, in the discussion forum, I interact with many students and encourage inquiry and interactive dialogues to help make the forum a place where meaningful interaction occurs. Sixth, I utilize Short Keys, a software that provides detailed and valuable feedback to students on their assignments. This tool helps me to focus on providing feedback that includes examples, ways to improve, and offers positive and constructive comments. It is also very efficient. Lastly, I also closely monitor the course email and respond quickly to any student questions because when a student sends an email in an online class, it is as though a hand has been raised, and I want students to know that their questions and concerns matter and are taken seriously. Overall, I truly seek to bring my residential teaching style and persona to the online classroom and treat it as though this virtual arena is as vital and important as any other classroom experience.

5. *How do you deal with at-risk students to ensure their academic success?*
   I reach out to at-risk students and meet in WebEx to show key course features. Also, it is so important to connect at-risk students to resources that can help them. Often, I will schedule a WebEx session and show students how to set up tutoring appointments or how to access the learning resource tools that can help them to succeed. I will send out email messages and contact students who are at risk to let them know that there are resources that can be useful

to help them to succeed. I send out the lecture archives and share article links and positive messages. Also, I encourage time management skills and, in live lectures and messages, I stress to students how important it is to manage their time and schedule while doing an online course.

6. *What do you believe are the most positive factors of online education? The most negative ones?*
The most positive aspects of online education are that learning is asynchronous so that students can work on their own time according to their own schedules. This is such an appealing feature for students who have full-time jobs, full-families, or personal lives. In addition, the skills that are utilized in online learning are transferable to the workplace and to career success. In the workplace, students will apply problem solving, information literacy, communication, time management, and digital fluency in their careers. These skills are necessary to be successful online. Online education can offer variety in terms of types of courses such as blended or fully online. Also, students can access lecture videos that can be replayed so that challenging material can be reviewed. For instance, students often comment that they watch parts of my live lectures a few times to make sure they understand all of the elements. This type of review and rewinding is not possible in a residential class. Through live sessions, students can have the best of both worlds they have live access to a professor, but also have the flexibility of online classes. Lastly, online education helps students develop self-motivation and discipline to stay focused on their courses and goals. The most negative aspect of online education is that students must be diligent and manage their time as they are not meeting with each other or the teacher face-to-face in a synchronous setting. This asynchronous setting requires more of the learning responsibility to be on the student. Without effective time management skills, it is easy for a student to get overwhelmed and feel isolated. Another negative aspect is that nonverbal communication skills are not as easily developed in online learning. This aspect can be overcome by encouraging synchronous attendance in online lectures or though the creation of video messages. Also, online education does not have as strong a sense of community as residential learning. The academic culture of online learning is not a built-in advantage. Each online institution must work to create an academic and dynamic student culture.

7. *What are the characteristics of a successful online learner?*
   Successful online learners have time management and organizational skills. Also, successful online students are self-motivated and take the responsibility of their learning very seriously. They have the confidence to keep trying when something is challenging, and do not give up easily. Online learning requires tenacity, perseverance, critical thinking, and determination.
8. *How would you personally improve the quality of online education?*
   Online education can be improved by offering as much interactive learning as possible. A curriculum that engages the student and activities that are incorporated to help scaffold student learning are key ways that I would personally like to improve for the quality of online education. By offering formative assessment activities that build skill level, students can build a strong foundation. Then summative assessment can offer students the ability to apply what has been learned through the use of authentic assessments.
9. *What future do you see for online education?*
   Online education has a very bright future. For example, blended classes are great ways to bring online learning and traditional classroom techniques together to merge the flexibility of online with the pedagogy of the residential class. I see a future where almost every class has an online component, because the flexibility of online and the access and resources that can be created online are just going to keep getting better and more engaging. We have the ability to make online learning state-of-the-art so that students can have a classroom experience that is like no other. Imagine that a student can log into a class and can learn about the Revolutionary War by virtually visiting the sites in places such as Boston, and hearing about events from a likeness of Patrick Henry himself. Online education can achieve this type of experience and take education to a whole new level.

Conclusion—Creating a Philosophy of Online Education

In her book entitled *Effective Online Teaching* (2011), Tina Stavredes ends her book with *her* philosophy of online instruction. The author makes many good points about her philosophy from a pedagogical point of view, but I would like to go one step further and end my book with a philosophy of online instruction that deals with what I call a student-centered focus of online education. Online education can be an education that is most convenient and affordable to many students, but remote and seemingly impersonal to many students as well, making online education a Hobson's choice for education: one that is really no choice at all, one that students make because online education is just there, with no other alternatives except more expensive, live education that has remained the same over the last several centuries. This handbook's goal was to demonstrate to potential online instructors that online education has the potential to educate more students and to educate them with as much of a personal presence as a technology-driven education will allow.

With this goal in mind, I propose a student-centered philosophy of online education. This student-centered philosophy encompasses all the aspects of online education (learning, technology, and professional development, to name the major areas), but primarily from the students' educational perspective. The ideal online instructor, whatever their professional or education background, devotes their time to ensuring that the students' education experience will become a rewarding and enriching one, and this devotion arises from a student-centered philosophy.

What consists of a student-centered philosophy? It is a philosophy that allows an instructor to be an educator and a mentor—while education and learning are the primary goals for the instructor and for the student, empathy plays a crucial role as well in successful online education. Empathy here does not mean pure emotion or allowing the student to take over the instructor's educational responsibilities (though students, of course, must and should be responsible for their education), but rather act as an instructor *and* a facilitator; an instructor who assists the student to reach their educational goals not only by book knowledge, but by emotional knowledge (or emotional intelligence) to ensure that students succeed.

With regard to technology, a student-centered philosophy ensures that instructors use the most communicative tools, such as instant messaging, videos, and live classroom lectures, to ensure that a technological bond with an online student is the most interactive and personable bond possible with an online education. The professional development for a student-centered philosophy ensures that online instructors remain as current as possible with online education trends and strategies, and can learn more from their colleagues through networking, whether live or online.

Online education has its proponents and opponents, and it is not leaving the educational landscape. It has its place alongside live education, and rightly so for its qualities that enable students to learn efficiently and effectively. Online instructors, by following a student-centered philosophy, will ensure that their students' educational experience will be a rewarding and successful experience.

REFERENCE

Stavredes, T. (2011). *Effective Online Teaching: Foundations and Strategies for Student Success*. San Francisco: Jossey-Bass.

INDEX

S

T

U

V

W

Y

9780081010136